## The Total Man Series

# THE HUMAN
# SOUL

## By Dr. Lester Sumrall

Unless otherwise indicated,
all Scripture quotations are taken from
the *King James Version* of the Bible.

*The Human Soul*
ISBN 0-937580-36-8
Copyright © 1984 by
Lester Sumrall Evangelistic Association
Published by LESEA Publishing Company
P.O. Box 12
South Bend, Indiana 46624

# Contents

## INTRODUCTION

This is a series of four books packaged together for your convenience, you can also purchase any of the four volumes separately.

This volume describes the human soul. It shows how the soul functions in its relationship in the human personality.

An automobile has 14,000 different parts. When they all perform in unity you have soft and pleasurable transportation.

When your total person is united in oneness with God you are happy, resourceful, and delight in sharing your success with others.

I have been more than twenty years studying the subject of the dividing or separating the human spirit and the human soul. In my search for truth I found little material on the subject. But of recent years there have appeared books and magazine articles on the subject.

It may not be possible to live a victorious and fulfilling life without pertinent knowledge of the total man, spirit, soul, and body.

# 1

# YOUR SOUL—
# THE ADAMIC NATURE

The human soul is the old creation of Adam. From the Greek word for soul, "psuche," we derive the words like "psychology," "psychiatry," and "psychoanalysis." They do not come from the born-again super-natural nature that God puts within us.

I Corinthians 2:14 says, "But the natural man receiveth not the things of the Spirit of God: for they are foolishness unto him. . ." Now it is hard to accept that, but it is true. You have a conflict within you with your soulical parts wanting to dominate your spiritual parts. Paul tells us in Romans that we have to fight it until we subdue it. If you are not careful, your Adamic nature will laugh at your born-again nature. You can accumulate all the facts and the information until you are a double Ph.D., but you will not know God through that. You will know God by saying, "Bring that spiritual born-again nature into me and revive the spirit part of me!" Immediately new things begin to come into your mind; new feelings begin to come into your emotions; and you become a new person in the Lord Jesus Christ.

## THE BATTLE FOR AUTHORITY

In your soulical parts are at least three dominant areas or "worlds." The first world of your soul is *the mind,* your thought center. No person has ever penetrated the depths of the abilities that God has instilled within the human mind.

The second tremendous element within you is your *emotional life.* Now these worlds are like chains. Sometimes you cannot tell where emotion ends and thinking begins, or where thinking ends and emotion begins, they are so intricately integrated within our inner being. Each person is a world of emotions. If you want some fun, get a long piece of paper and begin in the morning to write down every emotion you have all day long. You will be simply amazed by the emotions exhibited in only one day. You are an emotional creature. Emotion is beautiful when it is tied to your born-again nature, your spirit. If it is not born again, anger rises up within you like a lion; fear rises up within you to destroy you; hate rises up within you until your emotional world becomes dangerous. Unregenerate emotion can destroy you; it can destroy your family; it can destroy your business. You can come into your job with a sour face for a few days and your work will be finished. If you own the business, your business will be finished and you will be broke. You cannot bring a bad spirit and emotion into your business.

The third world of the soul is the area of decision, your *willpower.* Your will is a very remarkable thing. Again, the soulical areas are so interlinked it is difficult to tell where the mind and will finish and begin. In the will area of your soul, without God, a person can become stubborn and very difficult for anybody to get along with. Even the Lord Jesus said, "Not my will, but Thy will be done." He had to submit the will of his Adamic nature to the Father. He said, "I don't want my will." Your will can drive you to all kinds of bad situations, bad business, bad marriages, etc.

Now these are the three basic areas of your second man—your soul. This is the real you that you were born with. These soulical areas are never right until they are born again by the Spirit of God. We never feel right until we have Jesus in our hearts. Our emotions are never correct until we know God.

## LEARN TO SPEAK TO YOURSELF

Smith Wigglesworth told me, "I don't ever ask Smith Wigglesworth how he feels." I said, "Sir, you are Smith Wigglesworth." He said, "But Smith Wigglesworth never asks Smith Wigglesworth how he feels." What in the world did he mean? He was saying the same thing that David said. "Why art thou cast down, O my soul, Rejoice thou in the Lord." David was talking to David. The spirit man of David was talking to the soulical man David, saying, "David, you get up out of that gutter, stop being sad, and start rejoicing in the Lord. Get busy, rejoice in Jehovah!"

In many churches a third of the whole congregation is depressed and sad. They are people not living in the spirit; they are living in the soulical realm. Depression and sadness are not from heaven. God's kingdom, which is in you, is God's righteousness, God's peace, and God's joy. It has nothing to do with sadness and depression. If you live in your soulical parts and in your emotional parts, you are not living in your spiritual parts. Your spiritual part must command your mind.

Exercising your own will by making deliberate decisions of choice without God is living in the Adamic soulical parts of you in the volitional area.

## THE SOUL—"THE CARNAL MAN"

The soul of man is actually the center and the core of the human personality. It is the natural part. We call it the carnal part. It reveals man in what we can know of him—whether he has a sharp mind or not, what kind of decisions he is making, whether others can tolerate him or not, and his willpower.

The soul of man is seductive, deceiving, seeking its self-interest, and craving for carnal gratification. If you do not master it, it will never be subject to the Most High God. Some might ask, "Can't God do that?" No, God comes into your life and puts a spirit within you. The spirit within you deals with the other parts of your being, and you are responsible for it. God desires that only the spirit of man shall decide that man's destiny. What we call our human nature is the function of your soulical being. This is what you will have to struggle against in your spiritual life to be an overcomer.

Sometimes your soulical parts seem very

nice. You can be naturally a very gentle person, but the moment that you are not pleased, you will refuse to be gentle anymore. A man may walk into the house as gentle as you can imagine. He looks inside and seeing his wife kiss another man, he suddenly loses all his gentleness and becomes a raging lion. The veneer of your soulical parts in our civilization is just a thin covering. God is love and the attribute of God is love. Man, in all of his activities, will say, "I'm going to reach out there and be spiritual." But he cannot succeed unless he is born again. Man is not naturally gentle unless he wants to be. When he gets irritated, then he refuses to be.

When it's in trial, the force of human nature will react opposite to what you think your soulish nature is like. When you are suffering, when something goes against you, or when you are not pleased, your soul becomes something else. That is when people say, "Oh, that's not like me."

## SUBMIT YOURSELF TO GOD

The power and the abilities of the soul of man must not be destroyed. Jesus said, "I did not come to destroy, I came to fulfill." He does not mean to destroy the keen mind, the magnificent emotions, or the strong will. He did not come to destroy them; He came to use them in the kingdom of God.

If Hitler had become an evangelist and had used all the potential of his soul, he would have become the greatest evangelist that ever lived. He had the qualities there, but he would not allow Jesus to tame them. Many millions of people are like that today. When God, through the human spirit that he has placed within man, is allowed to rule human life, man can have a beautiful and successful life.

# 2

# THE WORKS OF
# THE SOUL

Man's soulish forces have been active throughout the millenia; not only the centuries, but the millenia. For example, it was man's soulical being which created and made the Tower of Babel after the Flood. This Tower of Babel that man conceived in his own mind was to be his own deliverance. He was trying to tell God, "Send the flood if you want to; we'll climb our tower and you'll never be able to get us." Man has always, with his mind, wanted to seek out that which God did not want him to seek out. The result of the Tower of Babel was about 3,000 languages in the world creating chaos, confusion, and conflict. Until this moment, tongues are a barrier. When you meet a person with whom you cannot communicate, there is a barrier there. Even if he speaks your own language but lisps when he speaks, or does not pronounce it according to your area, it becomes a barrier of friendship and many other problems may arise.

On the other hand, it was man's spirit, not his soul, that built Noah's ark. It was another building project. One was created out of man's soul and it created chaos. The other was created out of man's spirit, and it brought deliverance to the world. God is not against building. He is against building in the soulical parts, which have to do with your mind without God. On the other hand, the building of the spiritual parts has to do with doing things from God's point of view rather than the devil's point of view.

A very good example of this chemistry of the soul has to do with Israel's first king.

King Saul began by living and walking according to his spirit. I Samuel 10:6 says, "And the spirit of the LORD will come upon thee, and thou shalt prophesy with them, and shalt be turned into another man." Saul was to receive a new heart; this means he began in the spirit. He was to prophesy, which is of the spirit. Verse 7-9, "And let it be, when these signs are come unto thee, that thou do as occasion serve thee; for God is with thee.

THE WORKS OF THE SOUL

And thou shalt go down before me to Gilgal; and, behold, I will come down unto thee, to offer burnt offerings, and to sacrifice sacrifices of peace offerings: seven days shalt thou tarry, till I come to thee, and shew thee what thou shalt do. And it was so, that when he had turned his back to go from Samuel, God gave him another heart: and all those signs came to pass that day."

Saul was a man who began in the spirit. He began moving by the power of God. Anytime a person begins right, the devil does not want him to stay right. The devil wants you to get off in your humanistic manner of living. He wants you to go back into your Adamic principles of rebellion.

I Samuel 13:13, "And Samuel said to Saul, Thou hast done foolishly: thou hast not kept the commandment of the LORD thy God, which he commanded thee: for now would the LORD have established thy kingdom upon Israel for ever." When you live and are dominated by your soulical parts, the Bible says you are living foolishly. The Adamic nature is the spirit of rebellion. It is the separator from the living God, from peace in our hearts and from joy in our lives.

If you live in your soulical being, your

kingdom will not continue. God was seeking a man after His own heart. God went looking for another man. The Lord had commanded Saul to be the captain over His people. His eyes (his body) saw the wealth—the gold, silver, the beautiful raiment—and he wanted it. His soulical pride saw King Agag and he said, "I'll bring him back as a trophy." When Samuel met him, Samuel called it rebellion. In I Samuel 15:23 he said, "For rebellion is as the sin of witchcraft, and stubbornness is as iniquity and idolatry. Because thou hast rejected the word of the LORD, he hath also rejected thee from being king." Some people are willing to give God a gift, but they are not really interested in Him. They stay away from church or go somewhere where they should not go. They think that giving God a gift will calm Him down.

## THE RESULTS OF REBELLION

When this man revolted against God, notice what happened to him.

(1) According to the Bible he became depressed. He became so sad that his servants hired people to play musical instruments and sing in his presence, hoping to take the sadness away from him. Depression is not from God. It is a soulical condition that be-

longs to the human mind and has no relationship with God, with God's blessing, or with
God's power. When you are depressed, do not
blame it on God. God is not a depressor. Sin
and the soulical nature in rebellion against
God depresses people. Find out where your
depression comes from, and you will discover
that it has no relationship with the divine
precepts of God. It has no relationship with
loving and serving God.

(2) Hate against his successor came into
his heart. He believed David would take the
throne away from him and he began to hate
the young man. Hatred is a thing of the soul.
Hate is love gone sour. It is moving from the
spirit of man into the soul of man. The same
instrument with which you express love, you
show hate. The spirit within you that should
cause you to love moves over into the other
side to an area called antipathy and you begin
to hate. The Bible says hate gives birth to
murder.

Saul first took his javelin and tried to kill
David. Then he took his sword and went after
him in the field and said, "I will kill you." I
think it is very interesting to see how the
soulical parts work without God. First comes
depression, then hate, then murder, and finally
witchcraft. When he could not get anything

from God, he went over to the witch, and said, "Say, Gal, do you have anything from God for me? What is God going to do to me? Am I going to die or live?" That is how the soulical parts of a person can lead a person totally outside the will of God.

We have seen that the human mind is a department of the human soul. It is one of the most important parts of the human personality. Romans 1:28 says, "And even as they did not like to retain God in their knowledge, God gave them over to a reprobate mind, to do those things which are not convenient." Man without God, without the Bible, without the Spirit, has a reprobate mind inside of him. That is part of your soul. A reprobate mind is a mind that is in absolute anger and set against God. It has gone away from God and into the dirt of sin and confusion. It has to be changed by God's supernatural power to be anything else other than reprobate.

When a man will not be spiritual, he becomes carnal. There is no middle ground. Either you have a mind subject to the Spirit and the laws of God or you have a reprobate mind. There is no middle ground. We have to decide if we are going to function in our humanistic mind or in our divinely engrafted spirit. However, all too many Christians live in their reprobate minds. God has given them the new birth; yet rather than living in that Spirit, they have moved into rebellion saying, "I do not want to retain God in my knowledge whatsoever."

Romans 8:7 says, "Because the carnal mind is enmity against God: for it is not subject to the law of God, neither indeed can be." You are born with the Adamic mind. That is the reason you have the rebirth of the spirit.

It is not easy to study our inward parts. They are beyond our human vision and beyond our human hearing. On the inside of us is the inner man. This is the part we must really dissect and look into. We must say, "Where do all my actions and feelings come from?" They come from one of two sources— either from the non-born-again nature of your Adamic carnal being, or from the born-again nature where God puts into you His righteousness, His peace, and His joy. You are the deciding factor. You will have to decide whether they come up out of your spirit or up out of your soul. If they come up out of your soul, the Bible says they are carnal and not subject to the law of God.

## THE MIND IN WARFARE
## AGAINST GOD

Because of Adam, your natural mind has a hatred toward God. It is in warfare against God. It is not subject to the law of God, neither indeed can it be. No sinner can ever live in great peace with God. That is not possible. No unregenerate person can ever live in the glow of the spirit. That is not possible. You can only live in the spirit by being born of the spirit, and you can only walk with God when your feet are shod with the preparation of the gospel of the Lord Jesus Christ. So the beginning of the new man is a born-again experience. From there your spirit begins to dominate your life, and the power of God comes into you, and your mind becomes a servant rather than a king.

In Ephesians 4:17, the great apostle said these words, "This I say therefore, and testify in the Lord, that ye henceforth walk not as other Gentiles walk, in the vanity of their mind." The unregenerate person walks in the vainness of his mind. You only have to study human beings a very short time to see how tremendously real that verse is. The mind without Jesus, the Bible, prayer, and the moving of the power of the Holy Ghost, is full of emptiness, human vanity, and that which comes and goes. There is nothing permanent or solid about it. God wants you and me to live by our spirits and to live by the Holy Ghost within us. He does not want us to live in the vanity of the unregenerate human mind.

The Word of God says further in Colossians 2:18, "Let no man beguile you of your reward in a voluntary humility and worshipping of angels, intruding into those things which he hath not seen, vainly puffed up by his fleshly mind." Pride comes out of the old Adamic nature. Often we see a person with seemingly great humility telling others to worship angels, or denominations, or doctrines. They are actually puffed up in their fleshly minds and are not spiritual. This is where problems in churches come from. They come through the vanity of the inflated fleshly mind that has nothing to do with God. They are of the human nature and of the devil and have no relationship to spiritual things.

Psalm 94:11 says, "The LORD knoweth the thoughts of man, that they are vanity." God knows the thoughts of man. We might hide our thoughts from others, but not from Jehovah. God knows the thoughts of the unregenerate person. When He comes into you, He gives you a spirit. That spirit begins to cover your mind and says, "Mind, think the ways of God. Think the ways of purity. Think the ways of holiness, and I will fill you with good things, such as the Word of God, prayer, praise, and fellowship. I will fill you with these good things that will cause you not to have the vanity of being puffed up within your own mind."

In the Proverbs, the wise man Solomon said these words under the anointing of the Holy Spirit, Proverbs 15:26, "The thoughts of the wicked are an abomination to the Lord, but the words of the pure are pleasant words." In their human minds, the ungodly have thoughts that are an abomination to God. They are unreal and totally sinful before the Lord. God cannot accept them, and He will not accept them. If we want God to do something great and good for us, we have to determine, "My mind must be subject to God."

## WHAT IS THE HEART OF MAN?

The mind is an organ. It is a part of the soul, like other organs of the body. Death comes if it does not function. Proverbs 23:7 says, "as he thinketh in his heart, so is he..." As a man thinks all the time in his heart, as he dominates and promotes his emotions, *that is* what that man is.

In Jeremiah 4:14, God says, "O Jerusalem, wash thine heart from wickedness, that thou mayest be saved. How long shall thy vain thoughts lodge within thee?" God put the mind and emotions together. They are two soulical elements and are bound together like a chain. God put the two of them together so that your emotions and your mind function in unison. Your mind says it and your emotions do it. That is one of the other areas of your soulical being. Jesus said in Matthew 9:4, "Jesus knowing their thoughts said, Wherefore think ye evil in your hearts?" The human mind and the human emotions flow together. The mind says to the emotions, "Look angry; let your eyes look angry, let your face look angry, and let your words sound angry." Jesus said, "Why think evil in your hearts?"

He also said in Matthew 15:19, "For out of the heart proceed evil thoughts, murders, adulteries, fornications, thefts, false witness, blasphemies." These are the things that come up out of the great vast world dimension of the emotional part of the human being which is part of his Adamic nature. If this soulical nature is not controlled and dominated by the spirit, it will lead him the wrong way every time.

Genesis 6:5 says, "God saw that the wickedness of man was great in the earth, and that every imagination of the thoughts of his heart was only evil continually." God had to judge this wickedness with the Flood.

# 3

# THE CHEMISTRY OF THE SOUL

The Word of God says in I Corinthians 2:13, "Which things also we speak, not in the words which man's wisdom teacheth, but which the Holy Ghost teacheth; comparing spiritual things with spiritual." It has to do with that which is according to the earth, with the fallen nature. Men fall into lies very easily. Science and philosophy change all the time. At one time man thought the world was flat, yet God had spoken of the circle of the earth a thousand years before Jesus was born. Soulical men listen to man's wisdom but not to that which the Holy Ghost teaches comparing things with the spiritual world.

Verse 14 says, "But the natural man receiveth not the things of the Spirit of God: for they are foolishness unto him: neither can he know them, because they are spiritually discerned." A sinner cannot understand why you come to church. The Bible says it is foolishness to him because his spirit is dormant. He has no enlightenment in his spirit, and he finds it an impossibility to understand anything about spiritual things.

What happens to the heart and emotions of man when he gives himself over to God? If you live by your feelings, you are always going to be out of communication with God. However, we can have authority over our feelings. David, a thousand years before Jesus was born, spoke to his own soul and said, "Soul, rejoice." That was his spirit talking to his soul. David's own human spirit was talking to his own human soul. He was speaking to his emotions saying, "Emotions, feel good." Smith Wigglesworth told me, "I get up every morning and I praise and magnify God. I even dance before Jesus. My emotions are servants to my spirit, and that is what my spirit wants." The Word of God teaches us in Ezekiel 18:31, "Cast away from you all your transgressions, whereby ye have transgressed; and make you a new heart and a new spirit. . ."

God gives you new emotions when He gives you a new spirit. When the heart is under the direction of the spirit it is the holy, joyful, peaceful thing that God wants within the human personality. David's spirit controlled his emotions. Psalm 84:2 says, "My soul longeth, yea, even fainteth for the courts of the LORD: my heart and my flesh crieth out for the living God." I do not believe that there are many people like that today. David said so many revealing and enlightening things about worship. Psalm 122:1, "I was glad when they said unto me, Let us go into the house of the Lord." When the servant knocked on the door and said, "Oh, King, time for church," David must have begun to dance and said, "Oh praise God, Hallelujah, Jehovah! I'm ready! I'm ready! Let's go to the house of the Lord." He did not have the "mullygrubs" like some of us do.

His spirit was in dominance over his soulical parts which have to do with his emotional area. David made his soulical part subservient to his spiritual part. If we do not do the same, we cannot be what God wants us to be. We cannot be the light of the world until we get to be commanders of our soulical parts.

## YOUR EMOTIONS MUST BE UNDER THE DIRECTION OF YOUR SPIRIT

Job 23:16 says, "For God maketh my

heart soft, and the Almighty troubleth me."
He makes his emotions soft before him. If your
emotions get hard and mean and calloused,
you cannot be what God wants you to be. Your
spirit is born of God. Your born-again nature
that you received the day you were saved must
be the dominating factor in your life to make
your emotions obey. If you permit your emotions to be king they will drive you to the end of
the earth like a wild storm on the sea. Your
emotions are uncontrollable without the spirit
and the power of God.

Acts 4:32 says, "And the multitude of them
that believed were of one heart and of one soul:
neither said any of them that aught of the things
which he possessed was his own; but they had
all things common." In your emotions you
want to grab this and grab that. You want to
have this and have that. Emotion desires this
and desires that, but when the Church was at its
best, they were one emotionally. Everyone was
exalting and praising God for His wonderful
blessings and for His mighty power. They flow-
ed together in the Spirit. At that point, they had
the largest church the world has ever known.
The church in Jerusalem possibly had several
hundred thousand members in it, and they
were the people that had one heart and one
emotion before the Lord.

Colossians 3:22 says, "Servants, obey in all things your masters according to the flesh; not with eye-service, as men-pleasers; but in singleness of heart, fearing God." If you are going to serve, have a right spirit about it. There are a lot of people that work in a factory and all day long it is drudgery. If you live by your spirit, you can be just as happy with a screwdriver as you are with a songbook—if you want to be! You can be just as happy plowing a field as you are sitting in the pew—if you want to be!

If you let the devil say, "Oh, this is hard, I can't do this!", the first thing you know your whole being is going to be out of tune with God because you permitted your emotions to have their wild, Adamic actions. We need rather to have spirit-dominated actions by giving our emotions to God and flowing with God in our emotional beings. He says, "Not with eye-service as men-pleasers, but in singleness of your inner being." This means that our emotions are under the divine perogatives of God. Then it says, "fearing God," which only comes when we have the proper respect for God and know that God is God, and that we are just men.

Philippians 4:7 says, "And the peace of God, which passeth all understanding, shall

keep your hearts and minds through Christ
Jesus." God's emotion of peace surpasses all
human intellectualism. This peace will keep
your heart or your emotions. It will also keep
your mind and your thinking. Joy in your
emotions can flow up into your mind and
purify them and wash them clean and make
them sweet and blessed inside you.

## LIFE IS IN THE BLOOD

What is the human blood that flows
through your veins? It is like a river that
begins in the mountains and comes down to
wash away all the mess, the muck, and the
filth of humanity. The river puts them out into
the sea where God purifies the water with salt
and any other elements. He purifies it again
by lifting it up and vaporizing it, taking it up
into the clouds and dropping it again on the
mountain tops. Then it runs down again.
Rivers are God's cleansing system for the face
of the earth, and your blood is the cleansing
system of the body. The blood that flows
through you is a cleansing power.

The blood is the life flow of the soul and the
body of man. Leviticus 17:11 says, "For the
life of the flesh is in the blood. . ." Your life is
not in your bones or your muscles. Your life
is in your blood. God has given it to us upon

the altar for an atonement for your soul. This is done in order for your old nature to be changed, and for your old life to be renewed. When Jesus came, He had to give His blood because it is the blood that makes an atonement for the soul. Nothing else makes atonement. That is the reason the heathen still use blood. Witchcraft uses the blood of chickens and small animals. They use blood because the devil always counterfeits God. The devil has never been known to do anything original. He always counterfeits God and God has declared that your life is in your blood. It is your bloodstream that purifies your brain. Your brain must have a flow of blood or it will die. The blood flows throughout your body purifying, rejuvenating, bringing strength, and producing power.

The heart, the seat of your emotions, is the pump that sends that life throughout your whole being. That could mean that if you are wrong in your emotions, you are wrong everywhere. If you do not have your emotions under control, your whole person will be affected. The emotions of the heart are what projects the blood of life. Good emotions project life that makes you a new person, a new thing, and a new power.

We are not seeing the heart as the doctor

sees it, of course. We are seeing it as the contributing factor to your soulical personality.

## THE HUMAN WILL

The human will is so vast. Jesus was the master of His will when He said, "Not my will, but thy will be done." This is the supreme example of the spirit being alive in power and in authority. If the will is in rebellion, you are in trouble. Your soulical parts (your mind, emotions, and your will) are so important. We must look down inside of them and see what they are and know when they are functioning in God and when they are functioning in the Adamic nature.

I have heard of deacons saying in business meetings, "I'll have my way or I'll bust this church up." That is the human will under the direction of the old Adamic nature. It is unregenerated and without God. On the other hand, if the newborn spirit is within us, it will speak to our mind and say, "You be at peace with your fellow man." It will speak to your emotions and say, "Calm your words down." It will speak to your will, "Don't be stubborn; don't be a fighter; don't try to have you own way every time. Let the Holy Spirit dominate; agree with others, and let your will be subservient to God's will." When you live this way, you have the new man—the new nature, new power, and new authority. You have all the things that man needs to have a happy life and a beautiful life.

When we look through the Word of God, we can find so many that were rebellious in their willpower. There was Jonah. God said, "Would you go to Ninevah?" In his willpower, Jonah said, "I won't go. I'll make a decision. Ninevah is exactly east of where I am right now. I'll show you. I'll go to Spain." Jonah got on the boat to go to Tarsus. That was willpower—uncontrollable, suicidal willpower. That humanistic will breaks up homes. In order to have a happy home, each person's will has to be subservient to the other. You cannot say everyday, "I will do as I please today." You must say, "I'll do as the Lord wills today." God does not mean to make up your mind for you. He means for your will to live by your spirit. If you will live by your spirit, then you will be a spiritual person.

## BE SENSITIVE TO GOD'S DESIRES

Saul of Tarsus, who became the apostle Paul, shows us what it meant for his will to function. In the night he had a spiritual dream. In this dream he saw a man saying,

"Come over into Macedonia and help us."
That was a spiritual dream. When he awoke
in the morning Paul said, "I will." His spirit
was the king over his will, so he packed his little case and went the very next day. His will
was subservient to the call of God. To be what
God wanted him to be. No wonder he had
such a victorious life!

I was pastoring a great church in South
Bend. One afternoon the Lord spoke to me
and said, "Half the countries of the world
have only one big city. Touch that city for me
and you can touch the whole nation for me
with a great evangelistic center."

I said, "I believe it."

God said, "Then you go to Manila and do
it." I responded, "Get somebody else."

"No," He said, "You go."

"But I have a big church here."

God would not give in. "You! You go!"

My will inside of me wanted to say, "No!"
but my spiritual being said, "Tell your will I
said, 'Go!' Will, we're going." I walked right
downstairs to where my wife was cooking din-
ner. I gave her a big hug and said, "Honey,
we are going to live in Manila, Philippines!"

Now the thought of moving was as far from her as the East is from the West. She looked up at me and said, "Are we giving up our church that we've just built?"

"Yes, we are going to live in Manila, Philippines. You want to know something great? The Lord has said He is going to do more for us than He's ever done before."

She said, "Let's go."

I called a business meeting with the deacons and resigned, and shortly we left for the Philippines. That is the will working when it is submerged in God. The spirit said, "Go" and the will wanted to say "No." We said, "Will, you do not have anything to do with this. You just agree and go right along now."

If we let our wills be submerged in God's great love and power, life will be so much better. I can honestly and sincerely say that if I were to live my life over again I do not know where I would change it. Since I was 17 years old, I have lived in the will of God. Whatever God has told me to do, I did it. When God said, "Go live in Jerusalem," I took my family and we moved to Jerusalem. When God said, "Go live in Hong Kong," I picked up my family and we headed for Hong Kong. When the Lord said, "Live in Manila," I picked up my family and we went to live in Manila. When God said, "Return here," I picked up my family and came.

When Jesus taught us to pray in the Lord's Prayer, "Thy will be done, Thy kingdom come," Jesus certainly was pointing at the human heart. He knew it was an awfully strong area and He said, "Now when you're going to pray, pray this way. Pray for your human will to be broken down, that it will be subservient, and that it will not be rebellious like the devil. Tell your will to say, 'Thy will be done, Oh Lord.' "

God's will is perfect and good. He is not going to send you on a wild goose chase. The human element might, but when God sends us, we can be assured that all things will work together for our good.

Almost everything I have ever done in my life, I did not want to do in my natural sense. I did not want to preach, but I would be dead and in hell if I had not. I did not want to be a missionary, but I would not have been worth a dime to the human race if I had not. I was an evangelist, and I did not want to pastor, but I never would have blessed humanity like I have if I had not. I did not want to live in Manila after the war when three-fourths of the city was broken down and destroyed, with rats as big as cats running around. I did not want to live there, but it is the best thing I ever did for the country and for myself. The will of God is perfect. The will of God is good, and great. The will of God is a matter of rejoicing.

The human soul must become subordinate to your born-again nature. Romans 14:17 says, "For the kingdom of God is not meat and drink; but righteousness, and peace, and joy in the Holy Ghost." When God plants within you His holiness by the blood of Jesus, you are born again. He plants within you His peace and you have His nature. He plants within you His joy and you have His power and His authority upon the face of this earth. If these things rule in the human personality and they become the dominant factors of your total living, then the tripartite area of your soulical being (your mind, emotions, and will) begin to walk in the positiveness of the human spirit and you become great—great—great!

Moses was the meekest man on earth. This had to do with his soulical parts—not his great brain or his great leadership—but his soulical areas, his emotions and his will. When God said, "Turn right," Moses led the whole nation to the right. When God said, "Cross the sea here," he held up his rod and said, "Here we cross." His will was subservient to God. Everyone in the Bible, including Judas, who got out of tune with heaven, failed through his will. He was working in the fallen nature of man that began because of transgression in the Garden of Eden. If you live by your Adamic nature, you are going to live outside of the harmony of the Most High God.

# 4

# THE HUMAN MIND AND SPIRITUAL HEALTH

We want our spirits to be healthy; yet, our spirits can only be as healthy as the human mind is healthy. We read in I Peter 1:13, "Gird up the loins of your mind..." In Roman days men wore an outer garment that was a little long. If a man wanted to walk a little faster or run, he would fold up the skirt tail and tie a string around it. This was called "girding up the loins." A man only did that to establish a faster pace and to reach his legs out further. God says that you can take your loins, tie up and go. Your mind has this ability. If our minds have that ability, I would like to get mine girded up strong, in action, and going forward.

In I Corinthians 2:16 we discover that we

have the mind of Christ. What is the mind of Christ? If you have a mind like Christ, you have a strong mind. You have a mind that never knows fear. You have a mind that cannot be defeated. You have a mind that knows what is going to happen tomorrow. If we have the mind of Christ, we have a victorious mind. The greatest battle that you will ever have on the face of this earth will be in the area of your mind.

The passive mind is the mind that has no power of concentration. The passive mind finds it impossible to concentrate. When the devil interferes with the power of mental concentration he causes some people to become totally powerless in their concentration. They cannot memorize anything. Others concentrate in a flighty way. They can think of a thing for a moment or two and then their mind is off on something else. We can learn to cause our minds to develop powers of concentration so that we can stay on one thing as long as we want to. *We should discipline ourselves for it.*

The passive mind has to do with forgetfulness. There are some that are deprived of a power of memory. They forget what they just said or did. They cannot locate an article that they had in their hands five minutes before.

Natural loss of memory is an attack of the devil trying to cause our confidence in ourselves to go down. It causes our usefulness to be damaged.

## THE DEVIL WANTS TO DESTROY YOU

One of the ways or means of destroying you is through your mind. When we accept this as an attack of Satan, then we know how to fight the passive mind, we know how to resist it, and we know how to come against it. One of the instruments of a passive mind is what we call docility. The devil will take the person's mind and cause him to take opposite views very quickly. This is a very dangerous thing and you must discipline your mind for that. You must know what you believe and live according to the moral nature within you, you must be on one side or the other. If you take opposite sides to a thing very quickly, then you have a problem in your mind. The devil makes us to generate one kind of thought and immediately shifts us to another kind of thought and in that shifting admits the work of the adversary in our lives. A vacillating mind is the devil's tool. If you are on and off or you are up and down or you believe and then don't believe, the devil is playing with your mind. It is vacillating and the Word of God tells us that an unstable mind is like the sea. God wants us to make a decision and stick with it. If you know something, know it! If you believe something, believe it!

The unrelaxed mind is very dangerous. Insomnia is common in our country. It is the work of the enemy on the human mind. People say they lie down in bed endless hours thinking of all sorts of things. They count sheep and everything else and their minds are like machines that just will not turn off. Sometimes if you buy cheap gas for your car, when you turn the engine off it just keeps going. Some people's brains are like that. They lie down and turn to off, but it just keeps chugging. That can really hurt you. You will always find that this is from the devil. The Bible says the Lord gives his beloved sleep. There is only one thing that can happen to an unrelaxed mind; it will break. Many people in insane asylums today are there because of unrelaxed minds. We should have power over our minds and say, "All right you can relax now," and it will relax right there.

Many people commit suicide because they are not able to relax inside. They get all keyed up and they cannot stop. They just go until the devil destroys them. David in the 23rd Psalm wanted you to know forever that there is a place of tranquility and peace in God and it does not matter what happens to you. You can say to your mind, "Go to sleep now," and the mind has to calm down. You can command it to do so. If you cannot make it obey you, then you have a rebel working on your team, and you never know what the rebel is going to do. Anytime you want to go to first base, he may take off for third and you are going to have problems and sorrows. You must control your mind.

Many people let their minds do as they please. Their minds just run around and do anything they please. They have not disciplined their minds to think the things they ought to think and to do the things they ought to do. Your mind must obey because you make it obey. An unrelaxed mind is a tragedy. I cannot describe to you the people that I have met in my lifetime who had minds that would not relax. I am not talking about an occasional sleepless night, I am talking about a chronic condition.

If your brain starts playing games with you, talk to it. "Hey, brain, I have some news for you. I'm going to cause you to think right. Why don't you read Romans 8:1, 'There is therefore now no condemnation to them which are in

Christ Jesus...' " Unrelaxed minds have done much damage to a lot of human beings. Maybe they had no one to teach them, to help them, to pray with them, or to cause them to relax. I am a relaxed person and I am not keyed up and I do not ever intend to be keyed up.

## *LET JESUS RULE YOUR LIFE*

My whole life is going to be governed by Jesus. The things I do such as teaching and preaching, television work, and writing books, are all just going to be part of what I am doing. They have to all move together in the will of God and in the purpose of God. I will not permit any one thing to become a dictator over my life. I learned how to pray years ago. When I would kneel down, the devil began telling me things I ought to do over here and there. I could not get my mind on praying because of all these flashing thoughts. I said, "I'll take care of you." As I knelt down to pray, I put my writing pad right by me. Then I said, "Now, just give them to me and I'll write them down for you." When the devil saw that I was getting serious about praying and controlling my thoughts, he left. Sometimes there would not be anything on the pad.

You have to become the king of your mind. Flashing thoughts must not dominate and disturb you. Where there is a multitude of words there lacketh not sin. If the devil can get you to always be talking, then you are never listening and you will not learn much. There are some people who can be in the audience of a great man who may be saying something very important, but they are not hearing a thing he is saying. They are just waiting for him to pause so they can jump in and say something silly. The great thoughts of the teacher just drift through their minds like the wind, and they are all gone. Many people just talk and gossip and backbite and joke. A torrent of words run through their brains and mouths but nothing remains.

What happens to the mind at night in the subconscious or subliminal mind? Is there any hope of working on our minds during our sleep? I want to believe there is. I believe that when we pray before we go to bed we can take command of our minds. We can say to the devil, "You can't get in here tonight. No nightmares! If I have dreams, they're going to be sweet ones." Some dreams are inspired of God but there are others that are certainly generated by the devil. While there are some that produce psychic conditions, there are dreams which form part of the mental pictures that develop during the day. They come back to you in the evening times. During the night the brain is less active and the passive spirit of the brain can be manipulated. Sometimes the manipulation is by the devil. Some dreams cause men to wake up in a despondent spirit. Sleep did not replenish the strength within them. They say, "I got up feeling tired and miserable. I did not have any rest."

When you lie down at night, you must take command of your mind. I believe that we can cause ourselves to have sweet dreams and dreams of spiritual things. In nine out of ten dreams that I have, I am preaching and souls are getting saved by the hundreds and thousands. That makes me awake refreshed! I believe one reason for it is that I have commanded my mind that even while I sleep to refresh itself, to slow down, and to bring into being that which is inspiring to my total man.

Romans 10:5 says, "Moses describeth the righteousness which is of the law, That the man which doeth those things shall live by them." God wants us to live by certain principles. If you live that way, your mind will be that way. Ephesians 4:17-18, "This I say therefore, and testify in the Lord, that ye henceforth walk not as other Gentiles walk, in the vanity of their mind, having the understanding darkened, being alienated from the life of God through the ignorance that is in them, because of the blindness of their heart." We do not have to live with our understanding darkened, and alienated from the life of God through ignorance. God does not want us to be in such a condition. In salvation, man's mind undergoes a change. That is when you start working on your mind saying, "Now my mind is unshackled and is going to become empowered. It is going to become exceedingly active and have an amazing power of concentration." Paul said in essence in I Corinthians 2:16, I shall have, I will have, I must have the mind of Christ. I will have the mind of Christ. The mind can have spiritual health the same as your body. When I see a person's mind getting sick or disturbed, I am very upset inside. You can pray for a man's mental condition as well as you can pray for his fingers or any part of his body. God can touch his mind as easily as He can touch any other part of the body, and we shy away from that but we must not be afraid of it. God wants our minds to become strong and powerful, but more than that He wants them to become spiritual. He wants our minds to be the incubators of spiritual life flowing out to others. Our minds should be full of good and precious and wonderful things. God is able to make it so if we will yield our minds to Him and His spiritual truth. Anytime you close your mind off from a thing, you blind your mind. There are millions of people that turn their minds against spiritual truth. Your mind needs to be open and flowing. God is able to refurbish our minds every day. He is willing to both bless and strengthen our minds.

# 5

# SOUL IN CONTROVERSY WITH THE SPIRIT

The Bible teaches us that as a human there is a battle between what Adam was and what Christ is. You have the key. You can live either life.

Romans 6:7-8 says, "For he that is dead is freed from sin. Now if we be dead with Christ, we believe that we shall also live with him." That is the only way to get free from sin—die to it. Death does not only mean extinction. It can also mean separation. God said, "Separate yourself from this thing. Die to it!" If we are dead with Christ, we believe that we shall also live with Him. Water baptism is the signification of this truth. When you go down in the waters of baptism, you take your Adamic nature, your carnal nature, and submerge it into the waters. When you cover it over by the waters, that means it is buried. When you come up out of the waters of baptism, your spirit is resurrected. That is the spirit life.

Paul said, "I die daily." That old nature will rise up again and again, and you have to determine who will be the king of your life. If you are going to be an irritated person every day, your soulical part is the boss of your life. If you are going to say, "I'm grieved; I'm sad," you are permitting your soulical parts to be the boss in your life. If you wake up and say, "Hallelujah! It's a new day! I'm looking for about a dozen Goliaths," you are going to see some giants fall down and you will grow and increase. The spirit part of you will become great in your life.

Romans 7:22-23 says, "For I delight in the law of God after the inward man: But I see another law in my members, warring against the law of my mind, and bringing me into captivity to the law of sin which is in my members." Paul could see this controversy. If you study mankind you will also see this controversy raging almost every day. Man's soul, especially in his unregenerated state, is in a state of rebellion against his spirit. This controversy between spirit and soul includes such things as: *resentment, self-pity,* and *self-defeat.*

## DON'T DEFEAT YOURSELF

Did you know you can talk yourself out of every victory? You are not really defeated. You are self-defeated. This destruction comes from the wrong kind of a confession; "I cannot do anything today. I'm a failure. I cannot stand up to anybody." This is your soulical language. Did you know that you could take that same tongue and say, "I am a victor! I win all the battles! I'm going through!" This is the spirit talking.

There is a controversy between your Adamic nature and your born-again nature. You must win the battle. God is not going to win it for you. You must win the battle. I have seen some of the greatest people in the world who felt inferior to others. There was no rhyme or reason for it. It was Satan causing them to think so negatively. They were great; they had beautiful minds; they had beautiful personalities, but the devil said, "Oh, you're nothing. You can't do as well as others." These diabolical thoughts were dominating their lives. This is a soulical matter, not spiritual at all. In Jesus Christ we are more than conquerors!

You cannot imagine the people that go around condemning themselves saying, "I had a bad thought." No, you did not do it; the devil just put it in your ear. Tell him to get out of here and stay out!

There are millions of Christians walking around feeling condemned right now and it is a soulical problem. Romans 8:1 says, "There is therefore now no condemnation to them which are in Christ Jesus, who walk not after the flesh, but after the Spirit."

The human mind in its original state delights in those things which have to do with this world, that which is logical, or psychological. This is the realm of the soulish part. When we move in God, we move into another world of Spirit where God moves through our inner being and we know supernaturally what we ought to do. That is where God wants to live and be a victor in the controversy.

Maybe one of the classic references of the controversy between soul and spirit in the whole Bible is Joseph. Genesis 45:3-8 says, "And Joseph said unto his brethren, I am Joseph; doth my father yet live? And his brethren could not answer him; for they were troubled at his presence. And Joseph said unto his brethren, Come near to me, I pray you. And they came near. And he said, I am Joseph your brother, whom ye sold into Egypt. Now therefore be not grieved, nor angry with yourselves, that ye sold me hither: for God did send me before you to preserve life. For these two years hath the famine been in the land: and yet there are five years, in the which there shall neither be earing nor harvest. And God sent me before you to preserve you a posterity in the earth, and to save your lives by a great deliverance. So now it was not you that sent me hither, but God: and he hath made me a father to Pharaoh, and lord of all his house, and a ruler throughout all the land· of Egypt." The last time they had seen him they sold him for 20 pieces of silver. If your brothers sold you for twenty bucks and you became the governor of New York State and they came for some food, how would you treat them? The worst jailhouse would be the best place in town for them, wouldn't it?

The spirit of this man was so strong and so great. There is possibly no man in the Bible that excites me as Joseph does. He was mistreated most of his life. He was 7 years in jail for refusing to commit adultery, not because he did it. He had been mistreated since he was 17, and even after coming out of prison at 30 years of age, he still had a sweet spirit inside of him. That is what God wants of you and me. It does not matter how people treat you. Let your spirit prevail. Do not have self-pity. Do not talk about how you are mistreated and hurt. *Refuse to be hurt by any human being.*

There is a controversy in the world we live in today, and you will have to decide if you are going to let your spirit win or your soul win.

# MY CHALLENGE TO YOU

If you are not a Christian, I invite you to receive the hope and peace in your heart that only Jesus gives.

To become a Christian, you must deal with Christ Jesus directly. In a quiet moment, bow your head and talk to Him. In your own words say something like this:

*"Dear Lord Jesus, I am a sinner. I believe that you died and rose from the dead to save me from my sins. I want to be with you in heaven forever. God forgive me of all my sins that I have committed against you. I here and now open my heart to you and ask you to come into my heart and life and be my personal Saviour. Amen."*

If you say that to Christ and mean it, He will come in instantly. At once you will sense you have been transferred from the devil's dominion to the kingdom of God.

Read I John 1:9 and Colossians 1:13. A wonderful peace and joy will fill your soul.

If you pray a prayer like this, let me hear from you. I will send you a little pamphlet entitled, "So You're Born Again!"

Mail your letter to: **Lester Sumrall, P.O. Box 12, South Bend, IN 46624.**

61

*Other books by Lester Sumrall:*

*LeSEA Publishing Co.*
- Dominion Is Yours
- Genesis, Crucible of the Universe
- Paul, Man of the Millennia
- The Total Man
- The Human Soul
- The Human Body
- The Human Spirit

*Nelson Publishing Co.*
- Demons The Answer Book
- Grief, You Can Conquer It
- Hostility
- My Story To His Glory
- 60 Things God Said About Sex
- Supernatural Principalities & Powers
- The Cup Of Life
- The Names Of God
- The Reality Of Angels
- Where Was God When Pagan Religions Began?
- Jerusalem, Where Empires Die--
  Will America Die At Jerusalem?

*Harrison House*
- Faith To Change The World
- Gifts & Ministries of the Holy Spirit
- Jihad—The Holy War
- Unprovoked Murder
- Victory & Dominion Over Fear
- 101 Questions & Answers On Demon Power

Write for a free catalogue of all of Dr. Sumrall's books and teaching tapes: LeSEA Publishing Co., P.O. Box 12, South Bend, Indiana 46624.

For Visa, Mastercard or C.O.D. orders call 1-219-291-3292